THE IMPACT OF ENVIRONMENTALISM:
TRANSPORT

Andrew Solway

www.raintreepublishers.co.uk
Visit our website to find out more information about Raintree books.

To order:
☎ Phone 0845 6044371
📄 Fax +44 (0) 1865 312263
📠 Email myorders@raintreepublishers.co.uk

Customers from outside the UK please telephone +44 1865 312262

Raintree is an imprint of Capstone Global Library Limited, a company incorporated in England and Wales having its registered office at 7 Pilgrim Street, London, EC4V 6LB – Registered company number: 6695582

Text © Capstone Global Library Limited 2013
First published in hardback in 2013
The moral rights of the proprietor have been asserted.

Edited by Andrew Farrow, Adam Miller, and
  Diyan Leake
Designed by Victoria Allen
Picture research by Elizabeth Alexander
Illustrations by Oxford Designers & Illustrators
Originated by Capstone Global Library Ltd
Printed and bound in China by Leo Paper Products Ltd

ISBN 978 1 406 23862 4 (hardback)
16 15 14 13 12
10 9 8 7 6 5 4 3 2 1

British Library Cataloguing in Publication Data
A full catalogue record for this book is available from the British Library.

Acknowledgements
The author and publisher are grateful to the following for permission to reproduce copyright material: Alamy pp. 7 (© David R. Frazier Photolibrary, Inc.), 13 (© Caro), 20 (© Mark Boulton), 39 (© D. Burke), 51 (© AlamyCelebrity); Foster + Partners p. 52; Getty Images pp. 11 (Hulton Archive), 25 (Bloomberg News/Mark Elias), 37 (Bloomberg/Michele Tantussi), 41 top (Science & Society Picture Library), 41 bottom (Bloomberg News/Adeel Halim), 50 (AFP/ Frank Perry); © Greenpeace p. 14; Nature Picture Library p. 23 (© Ingo Arndt); Press Association Images p. 16 (Tim Ockenden/PA Archive); Photolibrary pp. 32 (Reso Reso), 44 (Lineair/Ron Giling), 57 (Ticket/Warwick Kent); Science Photo Library p. 35 (Matteis/Look at Sciences); Shutterstock p. 21 (© Dongliu); Siemens Press Picture p. 49; © Copyright United Technologies Corporation. Used with permission p. 27; University of Warwick p. 29; World Solar Challenge Australia p. 54.

Cover photograph of (top) exhaust fumes, reproduced with permission of iStockphoto (© David Parsons), and (bottom) electric trains in Zagreb, Croatia, reproduced with permission of Shutterstock (© bubamarac).

Every effort has been made to contact copyright holders of material reproduced in this book. Any omissions will be rectified in subsequent printings if notice is given to the publisher.

Disclaimer
All the internet addresses (URLs) given in this book were valid at the time of going to press. However, due to the dynamic nature of the internet, some addresses may have changed, or sites may have changed or ceased to exist since publication. While the author and publisher regret any inconvenience this may cause readers, no responsibility for any such changes can be accepted by either the author or the publisher.

CONTENTS

Words printed in **bold** are explained in the glossary.

TRANSPORT TODAY

Open up your fridge or storage cupboard and you might find beans from South America, apples from New Zealand, or cheese from Canada. Your shoes may have come from Vietnam, the family car could be from Japan, and your mobile phone from Finland. Without fast, cheap transport, we would not have any of these things.

We also need transport to move ourselves around. Many people live in the country and work in the city, take holidays abroad, and make regular trips to visit family or friends.

Concentrated energy

Nearly all our modern methods of transport rely on engines powered by fuels. The most important fuels are coal, oil, and gas, the three **fossil fuels**. Without fossil fuels, modern transport would not be possible.

Fossil fuels are very good sources of energy. They are easy to extract, they are fairly cheap, and they are available in huge quantities. However, fossil fuels also have serious problems.

Big drawbacks

Firstly, fossil fuels are not **renewable**. Once they run out, they cannot be replaced. In the past 150 years, we have used up huge amounts of fossil fuels. We could run out of oil, the most important fossil fuel, in the near future.

Secondly, fossil fuels produce polluting gases when they burn. The biggest pollutant is carbon dioxide. Carbon dioxide in the atmosphere acts as a **greenhouse gas**, trapping some of the Sun's heat. The extra carbon dioxide released from burning fossil fuels is making the Earth warmer. If carbon dioxide **emissions** continue, the world will get too hot for humans.

Peak oil

The petrol and diesel that fuel most of our transport are made from crude oil. However, oil is the fossil fuel that is most in danger of running out. Some experts think that we have already reached maximum production levels for crude oil. Many of the world's major oil fields are producing less oil than they have in the past – and new oil fields are not being discovered as quickly as old ones run out. It is getting more and more difficult to keep oil production at current levels. At some point the amount of oil we can produce will begin to fall.

The impact of environmentalism

Environmentalists are people who are working to slow down or stop our destruction of the natural world. In the 1950s, the environmental movement was very small, but it has since grown rapidly. Today millions of people are environmentalists, from students and scientists to politicians and pensioners.

Modern forms of transport have a great impact on the environment. Engines burning fossil fuels emit carbon dioxide that causes **global warming**. Other gas emissions cause pollution that kills wildlife, damages human health, and turns rain acid. The roads, railway tracks, docks, airports, oil refineries, petrol stations, and other structures that support the transport network also cause damage to the environment.

So what have environmentalists done to try and reduce the damage that transport does to the environment? And how successful have they been?

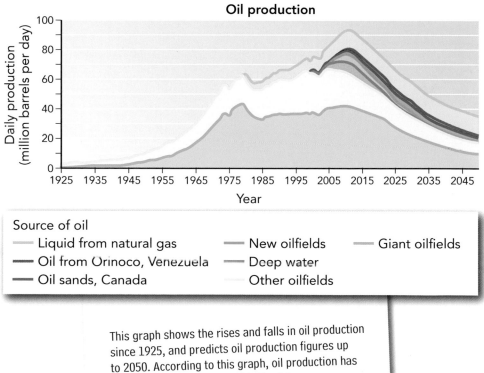

Oil production

Daily production (million barrels per day)

Year

Source of oil
- Liquid from natural gas
- Oil from Orinoco, Venezuela
- Oil sands, Canada
- New oilfields
- Deep water
- Other oilfields
- Giant oilfields

This graph shows the rises and falls in oil production since 1925, and predicts oil production figures up to 2050. According to this graph, oil production has already peaked and will fall in the future.

THE SCALE OF THE PROBLEM

If you have ever walked along a busy major road, or down a street where there is a traffic jam, you will have noticed some of the problems that transport brings. The air is smelly and unpleasant because it is full of the exhaust gases from the vehicles in the jam. The noise of the traffic is loud and sometimes deafening. You can feel big lorries making the ground vibrate as they rumble past. And the sheer numbers of vehicles on the road cause **congestion**.

Exhaust emissions

The emissions you see coming out of a vehicle's exhaust pipes are mainly solid particles of carbon – soot and smoke. These "**particulates**" are small enough to float and mix with the air, causing **smog** which can lead to human health problems.

The waste gases that you cannot see also are a big problem. Cars, vans, buses, and lorries produce a cocktail of polluting gases. Whenever a vehicle starts up, it begins pouring these exhaust gases into the atmosphere.

Burning is a chemical reaction of a fuel with oxygen from the air, so many of the gases formed are **oxides**. The most important of these gases is carbon dioxide. Transport produces about one-quarter of all carbon dioxide emissions. Other gases include carbon monoxide, a gas that can cause breathing difficulties.

Reducing particulates

Smoke and soot were much bigger problems in the past than they are today. Until the 1950s, the biggest source of particulates in Europe and many other countries was the smoke from coal fires. Smoke and soot from fires blackened buildings and caused smog and choking pollution.

In 1952, London was hit by the "Great London Smog". For five days, the city was covered in a thick, yellow-brown murk. During this time, deaths rose to three or four times normal levels. There were so many funerals that undertakers ran out of coffins and florists ran out of flowers. After the smog, the United Kingdom and other countries passed laws called Clean Air Acts to reduce the amount of particulates released into the air.

There are also oxides of nitrogen and sulphur that are the main causes of **acid rain**. Nitrogen and sulphur oxides are greenhouse gases, like carbon dioxide. They are part of the world's biggest pollution problem – warming of the Earth's climate.

The world's worst cities for particulate pollution (smoke and soot).	
City	Particulate matter (micrograms per cubic metre)
Ulan Bator, Mongolia	279
Cairo, Egypt	169
Delhi, India	150
Kolkata, India	128
Tianjin, China	125
Chongqing, China	123
Kanpur, India	109
Lucknow, India	109
Jakarta, Indonesia	104
Shenyang, China	101

The haze over the city of Los Angeles is caused by pollution from car exhausts.

Global warming

The effect of carbon dioxide and other greenhouse gases on the Earth's climate is called global warming or **climate change**.

The changing climate is already beginning to have some effects on the world's weather. The eight warmest years ever recorded have all occurred since 1998. The years 2005 and 2010 were the hottest years ever recorded, while 1998, 2002, 2003, 2006, 2007, and 2009 all take equal third place. There have also been particular hotspots. In 2003, a heatwave in Europe killed over 35,000 people. In the same year, 1,300 people died in a heatwave in India. In June 2006, there was another heatwave across Europe, followed by a heatwave across North America. In 2010, Russia had its worst heatwave in 1,000 years.

Not just warming

Scientists take millions of measurements at thousands of weather stations every year. These measurements show that, overall, the average temperature of the whole world is gradually rising.

Global warming does not simply mean that everywhere gets warmer. There have been some sizzling summers in recent years, but also some ice-cold winters. There have been droughts, but also heavy rainfall and flooding. This is because the climate may slowly be warming, but the *weather* can vary greatly from year to year.

However, extreme weather events do seem to be happening more frequently as the climate changes. Large storms, heavy rainfall, and long spells of drought are becoming more and more common.

Global effects

Climate change is already making itself felt. Some of the biggest effects have been in the Arctic and Antarctic, where ice fields, ice caps, and glaciers have already begun to melt. Sea level has risen about 1.8 millimetres per year for the last 100 years, and it will carry on rising for at least 100 years to come.

In the future, the effects of global warming could get worse. Millions of people could suffer from famine because of drought, while millions more may be made homeless by flooding. The changed climate will affect the **habitats** of many animals and birds, and some species will not survive the changes.

If we want to prevent the worst effects of climate change, we need to reduce the amounts of greenhouse gases we release into the atmosphere. This is one of the biggest challenges the human race has ever faced.

> "Climate change is the most severe problem that we are facing today, more serious even than the threat of terrorism."
>
> David King, UK Chief Scientific Adviser, 2004

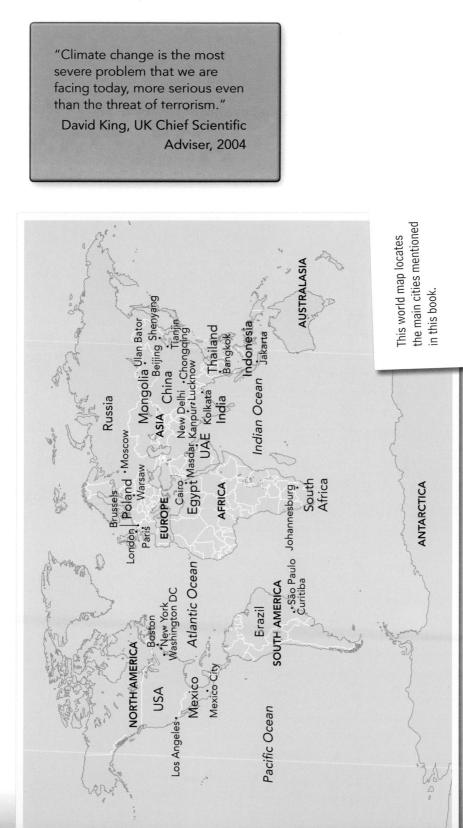

This world map locates the main cities mentioned in this book.

Other problems of transport

Polluting emissions are not the only problems caused by transport. Traffic in cities also causes congestion. Major cities around the world suffer from traffic snarl-ups. In cities such as São Paulo in Brazil or Beijing in China, jams can be up to 100 kilometres (160 miles) long. One traffic jam in Beijing lasted for nine days. Huge amounts of time and money are wasted as people sit in traffic on their way to and from work.

No.	City	Country
The world's 15 worst cities for traffic jams		
1.	São Paulo	Brazil
2.	Beijing	China
3.	Brussels	Belgium
4.	Paris	France
5.	Warsaw	Poland
6.	Mexico City	Mexico
7.	Los Angeles	United States
8.	Moscow	Russia
9.	London	United Kingdom
10.	New Delhi	India
11.	New York City	United States
12.	Johannesburg	South Africa
13.	Bangkok	Thailand
14.	Washington DC	United States
15.	Wrocław	Poland

Noise is another kind of pollution produced by many kinds of transport. Noise is unwanted sound. It may not seem like a very serious problem, but noise pollution makes people annoyed and stressed. Over time, it can damage their hearing. Road traffic is one of the most widespread sources of noise. Researchers have found that over 40 per cent of people are bothered by traffic noise. Fewer people are affected by aircraft noise, but it can be much louder and can even cause hearing damage.

Huge amounts of land and natural habitat have been destroyed to make room for roads, railway lines, car parks, and other parts of the transport network. As well as taking up space, roads and railways divide up the landscape. Many animals are killed crossing roads as they try to move from one area to another.

More people, more transport

In 1999, the world population reached 6 billion people, and it continues to grow. By 2099, the population is likely be around 9 billion. The transport systems in most cities and towns are already struggling to cope. Roads and railways are carrying far more traffic than they were designed for. As populations grow, this problem will get even worse.

Economic growth also leads to transport problems. As countries get richer, more people can afford to buy their own car and to travel on trains and airliners. So in countries with high economic growth, pollution and other problems due to transport are growing fast – even without population growth.

Then and Now
Old jams

Problems of traffic congestion and pollution are not new. There were horse-drawn snarl-ups in London and other European cities as early as the 1650s. Some were nearly as bad as today's traffic jams:

"Went this evening to see the illuminations, but the streets were so crowded with people and carriages that it was impossible to move. The throng was so great that I got to a lamp post and there I had to hang for half an hour before the road was clear that I could get [back on to the carriage] ... I went out at nine o'clock and got back at eleven. In that time I did not get more than half a mile."

William Tayler, 24 May 1837

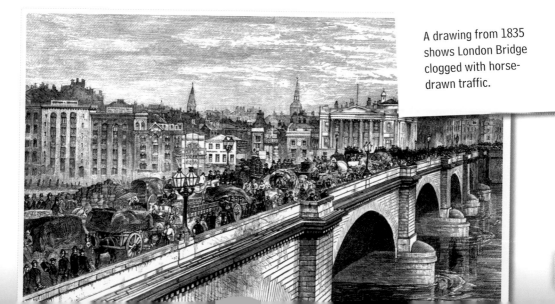

A drawing from 1835 shows London Bridge clogged with horse-drawn traffic.

PROVIDING THE POWER

For environmentalists, engines are the biggest problem with transport. But why is this? To find out, we need to look more closely at what engines do and how they work.

Engines can do amazing things. They can move over 10,000 tonnes of cargo from the United Kingdom to Australia, or fly 500 passengers across the Atlantic Ocean. Cars, trucks, boats, and aircraft are all powered by engines that burn fuel to produce **kinetic energy** (movement). There are two basic kinds of engine used in transport – **internal combustion (IC) engines** and gas turbines.

Controlled explosions

Petrol and diesel engines are IC engines. The "combustion" (burning) is an explosion of a mixture of fuel and air. This happens inside the engine in a small chamber called a cylinder.

When the fuel and air mixture explodes, it expands very quickly. The expanding gases push on a piston at the bottom of the cylinder and move it downwards. The piston turns a crankshaft, which goes round and round. Fuel and air go into the engine and rotary motion comes out.

Gas turbines

Jet engines are gas turbine engines. A turbine is a fan with many narrow blades. When a stream of gas flows through the turbine, it spins like a high-speed windmill.

In a jet engine, fuel and air are burned together in a combustion chamber. The hot gases from the combustion rush out through the back of the engine. The jet of hot gas shooting out backwards pushes the aircraft forwards.

Not all useful

Although engines are very useful, they have two problems that cause damage to the environment. The first is that most engines burn fossil fuels. We have seen that this is bad news for the environment because the burning fuel is turned into carbon dioxide and other polluting gases.

The other big problem with engines is that they are not very energy-**efficient**. A large amount of the energy used to fuel the engine is wasted as heat rather than being turned into movement. Three-quarters of the energy used to power an engine is wasted.

Then and Now
Early biofuels

Rudolf Diesel, who invented the diesel engine, fuelled his early engines with peanut oil. However, diesel oil made from petroleum was cheaper, so it soon became the most common fuel. Today, some cars can run on biodiesel (see page 32) which produces fewer carbon emissions than normal diesel. Biodiesel is made from plant oils – so diesel fuel has gone full circle.

Testing a jet engine. Jet engines can go through 3,000 litres (800 gallons) of fuel per hour. All the waste gases from burning this fuel shoot out of the back of the engine.

Go compare

A typical internal combustion or gas turbine engine is about 20 per cent efficient. How does this compare with other devices we use? Electric motors are far more efficient – an electric motor can convert about 85 per cent of the electricity it uses into movement. However, **incandescent light bulbs** are much less efficient. Over 90 per cent of the electricity powering a light bulb is wasted as heat.

NOTICING THE PROBLEM

Air pollution was the first environmental problem linked to transport to get noticed. In the 1950s, the UK government introduced a Clean Air Act to try and reduce air pollution. The act was aimed mainly at reducing the amount of soot coming from factories and coal fires. However, in 1960, investigators in the United States looked at the causes of smog in large cities such as Los Angeles. They found that much of the pollution was caused by gases from car exhausts. In 1963, the US government passed its own Clean Air Act aimed at trying to control the pollution from car exhausts. It was one of the first attempts to try and stop the environmental damage caused by cars and other transport.

Environmental activists from Greenpeace protesting against pollution today. Oil can be extracted from tar sands like these in Canada, but it involves cutting down large areas of forest, and the process produces large amounts of carbon dioxide.

The environmental movement starts

The environmental movement was already quite strong in the United States by the time the Clean Air Act was passed. It began in the mid-1800s, when a few people began to object to the way that humans were damaging the natural environment. American environmental pioneers, such as John Muir and George Perkins Marsh, were involved in establishing national parks – unspoiled wilderness areas that were protected to maintain the natural habitat.

By the start of the 1960s, there were national parks in many countries. Environmentalists were mainly concerned with protecting natural areas and wildlife. Most people still knew very little about environmental damage or pollution of the air and water.

Then and Now
Muir and Marsh

John Muir and George Perkins Marsh both lived in the 1800s, but their ideas are still relevant today.

Muir was a naturalist who wanted to protect wilderness areas in the United States. He founded one of the first-ever environmental organizations, the Sierra Club. Its aim was to "explore, enjoy, and protect the wild places of the Earth". He also helped to found Yosemite National Park. The modern science of **ecology** has shown that the animals and plants living in a habitat are interconnected in a complex web. Muir recognized this before ecology had been invented. He said, "When one tugs at a single thing in nature, he finds it attached to the rest of the world".

Marsh wrote one of the first books on ecology, called *Man and Nature*. He argued that cutting down forests would lead to erosion and degrading of the soil. This is just what has happened where areas of rainforest have been cut down.

A wider audience

During the 1960s, people became more aware of the effects of pollution, especially in the United States. US cities such as New York City and Los Angeles suffered from smogs as bad as those in London. The Cuyahoga River in Ohio, USA, caught fire because there was so much pollution in the water.

In 1967, the *Torrey Canyon* oil tanker sank off the coast of Cornwall, causing one of the first major oil spills. And a book called *Silent Spring*, by the US biologist Rachel Carson, showed how a **pesticide** called DDT was poisoning wildlife in many parts of the world. *Silent Spring* became a bestseller, and it made millions of people aware of how human actions could cause environmental problems.

Taking action

By the end of the 1960s, the environmental movement had grown very large. The Earth Day protests in the United States showed just how many people were worried about pollution and the environment. The first Earth Day took place on 22 April 1970. Over 20 million Americans took part in demonstrations and marches across the country. College students went to lectures in gas masks to highlight the problems of air pollution. School students picked up litter from the streets, and some New York City streets were closed to all cars. Over a million people gathered for the Earth Day rally in Central Park in New York City.

Not all environmental protests have an impact. In 1996, many protesters in the UK tried to persuade planners to change the route of a bypass around Newbury in Berkshire – but the road was built as planned.

The environmental protests were large, and they did have some effects on transport. There were many protests in the United States and Europe against the building of large roads, and some road-building projects were abandoned. But it was another event, which had nothing to do with environmentalists, which led to the first real moves away from fossil fuels in transport.

Then and Now
Different protests

Environmentalists supporting the first Earth Day were protesting about many different things. Many of their concerns were the same as those of environmentalists today. They wanted power stations to reduce the amounts of polluting gases they were pumping into the air. They wanted mining companies, oil producers, and chemical factories to stop dumping toxic waste materials that could poison the environment. They were worried about oil spills from large tankers, and the loss of wilderness areas. But there was one big difference from environmental concerns today. There were no large protests against global warming. This was because, in the 1960s, the problem of global warming was only just being recognized.

Making an impact

Since the 1960s, environmentalists have been less successful in actually stopping road-building projects. However, environmental arguments do often influence the routes of roads and where airports are built. Today, any new road or airport needs an environmental impact assessment that shows how the road or building will affect the environment and how the negative impact can be kept to a minimum.

ENVIRONMENTALISM IN ACTION

The energy crisis

In the early 1970s, environmentalists protesting about transport were concerned about the increasing numbers of cars on the road, the numbers of new roads being built, and the particulate emissions that caused smogs. Few people concerned about the environment were worrying about reducing carbon dioxide emissions and reducing fossil fuel use.

Crude oil was the most important fossil fuel at the time. We relied on oil even more than we do today. So when there was a hiccup in the oil supply in October 1973, it shook the world.

A political argument

The oil crisis was the result of a political argument between the United States and Arab countries in the Middle East. The Middle East countries are the biggest oil producers in the world. They are members of the Organization of Oil Exporting Countries (OPEC).

In 1973, the United States was supporting Israel in a war with the Middle Eastern countries Syria and Egypt. Because of this support, the Arab members of OPEC decided to stop selling oil to the United States. At the same time, they increased the price of oil to Europe, Japan, and other rich countries by 70 per cent.

Shortages and rationing

The oil crisis quickly had serious effects – especially in the United States. The United States is a big oil producer, but it uses even more oil than it produces. In the 1970s nearly all this oil came from the Middle East. Within a few days there were queues at petrol stations. By early 1974, 20 per cent of US petrol stations had no fuel at all.

The US government brought in rationing to try and cut queues at the petrol pumps. Cars with number plates that ended in an odd number could buy petrol on odd-numbered days, while number plates with even numbers could only fill up on even-numbered days.

"America is addicted to oil, which is often imported from unstable parts of the world. The best way to break this addiction is through technology."

US President George Bush, 2006

What is oil?

Crude oil is a liquid mixture of **hydrocarbons** that is found underground. The different parts of the crude oil mixture are separated in an oil refinery.

Crude oil is the most important fossil fuel. Petrol, diesel, and aviation fuel are all extracted from oil. Fuel oil powers most of our electricity production and is a major heating fuel.

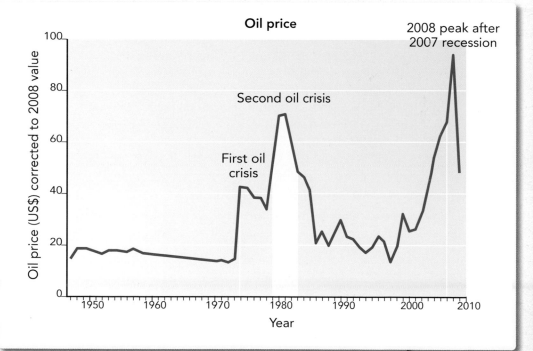

The changes in the average price of crude oil since 1947. The peaks in oil prices during the 1970s and 1980s were caused by the first and second oil crisis, but the reasons for the huge spike in oil prices during 2008 are unclear.

Longer-lasting effects

After only a few months, the United States and Arab OPEC members sorted out their political problems and the oil supply to the United States resumed. However, the crisis showed the oil-producing countries how powerful they were. Oil prices remained high for most of the 1970s, and there was a second oil crisis in 1979.

The high oil prices led the United States and other rich countries to look for ways to reduce their reliance on oil. When oil was cheap, many Americans drove large cars that used lots of fuel. These "gas-guzzlers" were replaced by smaller, more efficient vehicles. Governments also encouraged research into solar power, electric vehicles, and other renewable alternatives to oil. In Brazil, the government began making an alternative to petrol from sugar cane (see page 33).

Then and Now
The CitiCar

In 1974, a US company called Vanguard-Sebring produced an all-electric, two-seater car called the CitiCar. Its motor produced 3.5 horsepower, it had a top speed of 64 kilometres (40 miles) per hour, and it needed recharging after about 65 kilometres. It was light and did not rust. The CitiCars sold in their thousands, and Vanguard-Sebring became the sixth biggest car maker in the United States. However, as the oil crisis faded, the car lost popularity and the company went out of business.

In 1974, the all-electric Vanguard-Sebring was one of the best-selling cars in the United States.

The impact of environmentalism

The oil crises of 1973 and 1979 probably did more than anything else to kick-start research into alternatives to fossil fuels. Environmental concerns were not the main reason behind decisions to build electric cars and develop solar power. However, environmentalism has had some impact. The research that began in the 1970s could have stopped once oil supplies were restored. But broader concerns about the environment meant that the research continued into the 21st century. The results of this research are an important part of much of today's "green" technology.

In recent years, a few all-electric cars have begun to appear. One example is the Nissan Leaf, which went on sale in the United States and Japan in 2010. The Leaf is a four-seater that looks and feels like any family car. The motor produces 110 horsepower, and the car has a top speed of 150 kilometres (93 miles) per hour. Because it uses an electric motor, the Leaf needs no gears. It can accelerate strongly at any speed, which makes it feel very lively to drive. However, it has a maximum range of only 160 kilometres (100 miles) before it needs to be plugged into the mains for several hours for recharging.

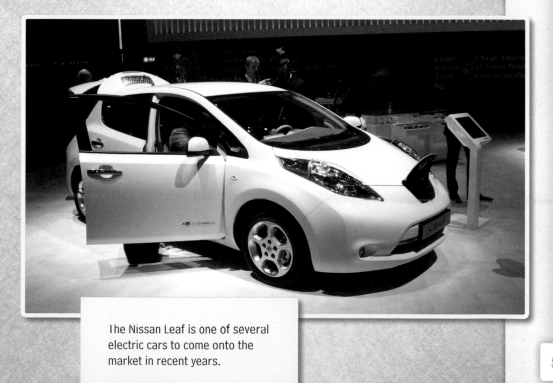

The Nissan Leaf is one of several electric cars to come onto the market in recent years.

SUSTAINABLE DEVELOPMENT

In the 1980s and 1990s, many people forgot about the oil scares of the 1970s, but scientists were finding more evidence for global warming and environmental damage.

In 1983, the United Nations set up the World Commission on Environment and Development to look at what could be done about the growing problems of the planet. The commission produced a report in 1987 called *Our Common Future*, or the Brundtland Report. It suggested practical ways in which we could reduce pollution and damage to the environment.

Our Common Future identified many environmental problems facing the world. The report concluded that the richer countries were using up the Earth's resources more quickly than they could be replaced or renewed. What was needed was **sustainable** development.

Sustainable development: the aims

The world economy is currently based on economic development. This means that countries try to increase the amount of money they make from selling **goods** (things they make) and services (things they do, such as banking, nursing, or hairdressing).

Sustainable development takes a longer-term view of the Earth and its resources. According to the Commission on Environment and Development: "Sustainable development is development that meets the needs of the present without compromising the ability of future generations to meet their own needs". Some of the ways of improving sustainability include recycling materials and using energy resources that are renewable, such as solar or wind power. But for transport, one of the most important improvements has been making vehicles more efficient.

Government targets

In the years since the Brundtland Report, governments of countries around the world have begun to take the issue of climate change and global warming seriously. Today, most countries have targets for reducing their carbon emissions. The UK government has pledged to cut carbon emissions to half their 1990 levels by the year 2025. The emissions from transport will certainly have to be reduced to help meet this target.

An ice core being drilled in the Arctic. Scientists can use ice cores to get information about past climates, stretching back thousands of years. This kind of evidence has helped to show that human actions are changing the world climate.

Our Common Future

The main point of the Brundtland Report was that we are using up the planet's resources so quickly that the natural environment cannot recover and renew itself. The effects of this "spendthrift" behaviour will be felt by our children and grandchildren rather than by people living today. A quote from the Brundtland Report made this point very clearly:

"We borrow environmental capital from future generations with no intention or prospect of repaying. They may damn us for our spendthrift ways, but they can never collect on our debt to them. We act as we do because we can get away with it: future generations do not vote; they have no political or financial power; they cannot challenge our decisions."

Improved efficiency

Despite the findings of the Brundtland Report, we continue to use fossil fuels to power cars, trains, aircraft, and other vehicles. However, there has been one major improvement: most of the engines that power these vehicles are more efficient than they were in the 1980s.

We saw on page 12 that engines are not very efficient. They are not very good at turning the chemical energy from fuel into kinetic energy. Some of this inefficiency is "built in". It is not possible for an engine of this kind to be 100 per cent efficient, even in theory. However, it has proved possible to make substantial improvements in engine efficiency.

The move to diesel

There have been many changes that have improved efficiency. One of the most important has been the shift to diesel cars. Diesel engines use nearly one-third less fuel than petrol engines.

In the 1970s, diesels were dirty and noisy. They were used only in trucks. Today's diesel engines are quieter and more efficient. They are often turbocharged (see opposite), which gives them better power and acceleration. Modern diesel fuels are much cleaner than in the past. Also, filters fitted to the exhaust prevent soot and other particulates from escaping into the air.

All these improvements, plus their better fuel consumption, have made diesel cars increasingly popular. In 2010, sales of diesel cars in the United Kingdom overtook petrol car sales for the first time.

Future developments: six-stroke engines

Most petrol and diesel engines today are four-stroke engines. This means that there is one power stroke (combustion) for every four piston strokes (down, up, down, up). However, several types of six-stroke engine are currently being developed. Early tests suggest they could be 40 per cent more efficient than a similar four-stroke engine.

The BMW X6 is not a "green" car. It is heavy and powerful, with a large, 3-litre engine. However, the start–stop system and regenerative braking reduce fuel consumption and save battery power.

Other improvements

Many other improvements since the 1970s have helped to make car engines more efficient.

• *Fuel injection:* In the 1970s, most cars had carburettors, where fuel and air were mixed before they were sprayed into the cylinder. Today, fuel injection systems mix fuel and air more accurately without the need for a carburettor.

• *Turbos and superchargers:* These are types of fan that compress the air going into the engine cylinders. With compressed air, the explosion of the fuel gives more power. An engine with a turbocharger or supercharger can be smaller than a non-turbo version and produce the same power.

• *Start–stop system:* Energy is wasted when a car is stopped with the engine idling. Start–stop systems automatically stop the engine when it has been idling for a second or two, then start it up again when the driver presses the accelerator.

• *Regenerative braking:* When a car brakes, its kinetic energy is usually lost as heat in the brakes, through friction. With regenerative braking, some of the kinetic energy is used to power a generator. This means that braking charges the battery rather than heating up the brake pads.

Better jets

The fuel efficiency of jet engines has improved even more than that of petrol and diesel engines.

In the first jet engines (**turbojets**), all the air drawn in by the compressor went into the combustion chamber and came out of the engine as hot gas. Modern airline engines are known as "high-bypass" jets, because most of the air passes around the combustion chamber rather than going through it. The bypass air absorbs heat from the combustion chamber as it flows round it. This heat would otherwise be lost into the atmosphere. The jet of gas coming out of the back of the engine is a mix of warm bypass air with very hot combustion gases. A high-bypass jet gives more thrust (forward "push") than a turbojet of the same size.

Efficient turbofan engines work best in modern airliners, which spend most of their time cruising. Military jets are far less efficient, because they need to produce more thrust. To do this, less of the air going into the engine is bypassed round the combustion chamber. For sudden bursts of speed, military jets have an afterburner. This is a mechanism for burning fuel at high temperatures in the jet exhaust. Afterburners give a lot of thrust, but they are very inefficient.

Higher emissions

Transport today is much more energy-efficient than in the 1970s. Despite this, the carbon emissions from cars and other vehicles are much greater now. There are two main reasons for this.

The first reason is that there are many more cars on the roads. In 1969, just before the oil crisis, there were around 217 million cars on the road. Today the number has almost tripled, to around 600 million. Passenger air miles flown increased from around 12 billion in 1973 to over 800 billion in 2010.

The second reason is that we expect much more from cars today than we did in the past. In the 1970s, only top luxury cars had features such as power steering and air conditioning. Today, they will be fitted as standard on even a fairly basic family car. Safety standards are also much higher for modern cars, which must have features such as side-impact bars and crumple zones to protect the driver and passenger. These extra features make cars heavier and use extra energy.

Future directions

A new kind of turbofan developed by US engine makers Pratt & Whitney could make big reductions in carbon emissions from jet aircraft. In a normal turbofan engine, the large turbine that draws in air at the front of the engine turns at the same speed as the much smaller turbine that compresses the air going into the combustion chamber. However, it would be more efficient if the large turbine could turn at slower speeds and the small compressor could turn much faster. The Pratt & Whitney PurePower® engine is a new kind of engine called a geared turbofan. It has a gearbox between the large and small turbines, so that they can both turn at optimum speeds.

This is the Pratt & Whitney PurePower® engine. It is a shorter, lighter engine that can produce the same amount of power using 12–15 per cent less fuel.

ENVIRONMENTALISM IN ACTION

Cutting down waste

In one particular way, cars have always been friendly to the environment. Most of the materials in them have always been recycled. A car or other vehicle contains large amounts of steel, some aluminium, lead, and other valuable metals. All these metals can be separated from each other, melted down, and used again. There is a huge worldwide industry involved in breaking up damaged vehicles and separating the different metals in them for recycling.

Scrap dealers buy used cars and break them up because they can make money from selling the scrap metal. However, recycling also gives a big environmental advantage. A car or other vehicle is a complex piece of machinery that takes a lot of energy to make. More often than not, this energy comes from fossil fuels. If the materials from a car are recycled we get some of this energy back. And every tonne of steel or other metal reclaimed from a car saves having to dig up and extract a tonne of metal from rock.

The more of a car that can be recycled, the more energy it saves. The easiest material to recycle is steel. However, the amount of steel in cars is getting less. In the 1970s, about 87 per cent of a car was steel. A modern car is only about 65 per cent steel. Lighter materials, such as aluminium and plastics, have replaced some of the steel. Aluminium can be recycled, but plastics are difficult to reuse and usually end up in landfill.

Many manufacturers have tried to make more of their cars recyclable or **biodegradable**. Two kinds of material have been used instead of plastics. The first are materials that are made from recycled waste. Volkswagen, for example, are processing plastics, glass, textiles, and rubber from old cars and using them again.

The other approach is to make new kinds of plastic that are made from plant material instead of from oil. These kinds of **biomaterials** have two advantages. First, they are sustainable because new plants can be grown to replace those used to make plastics. Second, bioplastics are biodegradable. They break down into simple materials and are naturally recycled in the environment.

What's next?

Researchers at Warwick University have built the World F3rst, a car that shows just how much can be done towards making cars more environmentally friendly. It is a full-blown racing car, with a top speed of 240 kilometres (150 miles) per hour, using sustainable materials.

Many parts of the car are made from biomaterials. The front spoiler is made from potato **starch** and some other body parts are made from hemp and flax fibres. The steering wheel is a kind of plastic made from carrots. Other body parts are made from recycled materials. The engine runs on a **biofuel** (see page 30) made from waste chocolate, and it is lubricated by plant oils.

The World F3rst racing car is the first ever racing car to be built largely from sustainable materials.

GREENER FUELS

By the 1990s, scientists and environmentalists had put together a convincing argument to show that carbon dioxide emissions from burning fossil fuels were causing climate change. Governments began to take the problem seriously.

In 1992, more than 100 world leaders met in Rio de Janeiro, Brazil, for the first Earth Summit. Their aim was to address the Earth's urgent environmental problems, particularly climate change. Many countries signed a treaty called the Framework Convention on Climate Change (FCCC). This was an agreement that countries would work together to keep greenhouse gases in the atmosphere down, and so avoid dangerous warming of the planet.

In 1997, at the second Earth Summit, 191 countries signed up to the Kyoto Protocol. This involved countries promising to reduce their carbon emissions to specific levels by 2012.

After 1997, governments began to look for ways to reduce their carbon emissions. One way to reduce emissions from transport looked very promising. This was to replace fossil fuels with biofuels.

What are biofuels?

Fossil fuels are the remains of plants and animals that died millions of years ago. These remains were squashed and heated below ground for long periods. Eventually they formed oil, gas, or coal.

Living plants and animals have the same basic ingredients as fossil fuels. So with some careful squashing and cooking, it should be possible to use plants or animal wastes to make fuels. Fuels made this way are called biofuels.

Big advantages

Biofuels have some big advantages over fossil fuels. First, they are a renewable energy source. If we make biofuel from sugar cane, for example, it is not a one-off process. We can grow a new batch of sugar cane every year. Another advantage is that biofuels can be made locally. Some countries are rich in fossil fuels, while others have hardly any. But any country can grow crops or use waste materials to make biofuels.

The biggest advantage of biofuels is that, in theory, they produce fewer carbon emissions than fossil fuels.

Biofuels in theory

Fossil fuels and biofuels produce similar amounts of carbon dioxide when they burn. So how can a biofuel produce fewer emissions? To understand, we need to go back to when the biofuel crop is planted. Like any plant, the fuel crop makes its food by photosynthesis. In this process, the plant combines carbon dioxide and water, using light energy from the Sun, to make sugars. The sugars are used to fuel the plant's growth. So, all the time it is growing, the plant is absorbing carbon dioxide from the atmosphere and turning it into plant material.

When the biofuel crop burns, it emits carbon dioxide. However, the carbon emissions are offset by the carbon dioxide that the plant absorbed while it was growing.

Biofuels for aircraft

Researchers have recently begun tests on using biofuels in aircraft. The first test flights using biofuels were made in 2010. In 2011, the airline Lufthansa made the first commercial flights using biofuels. European airlines plan to be using 50 per cent biofuels by 2040.

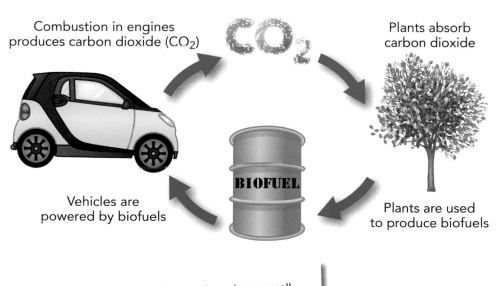

Combustion in engines produces carbon dioxide (CO_2)

Plants absorb carbon dioxide

Vehicles are powered by biofuels

BIOFUEL

Plants are used to produce biofuels

This diagram shows how, overall, biofuels recycle carbon dioxide.

Types of biofuel

There are several different types of biofuel.

Bioethanol: Bioethanol is alcohol made from plants. Alcohol burns in a similar way to petrol, so petrol engines can be modified fairly easily to use bioethanol. The two biggest bioethanol producers are the United States, which makes bioethanol from maize (corn), and Brazil, where bioethanol is made from sugar cane.

Biodiesel: Biodiesel is made from plant oils or animal fats. It can be used as a replacement for diesel fuel with minimal changes to the engine. At present, most biodiesel is made from soybean oil, palm oil, or rapeseed oil. However, some biodiesel plants can use different kinds of oils and fats, such as waste animal fat from **abattoirs**.

In Linköping, Sweden, the local train and a fleet of buses run on biogas. This biofuel is made from animal waste from local abattoirs.

Biogas: Biogas is gas produced by **fermenting** animal wastes or other organic material. In fermentation, the waste material is kept warm in a closed container. Bacteria and other microbes "eat" the waste, and biogas is produced. Biogas is a mixture of methane (natural gas) with other gases. The methane can be purified and used as a transport fuel, but the vehicles have to be specially built to run on gas.

Two types of biofuel

The same biofuel produced in different ways can produce very different carbon emissions.

In the 1970s, Brazil began making bioethanol from sugar cane. All the fuel for cars sold in Brazil since 1976 has been a mixture of bioethanol and petrol. The cars have "flexfuel" engines that are designed to run on a mixture of the two fuels.

Bioethanol production in Brazil is very efficient. Sugar cane grows without the need for fertilizers or other chemicals. It produces a large amount of biofuel per hectare of land on which it is grown, and the waste from processing (a material called bagasse) can be used as a heating fuel. Bioethanol produced this way has carbon emissions that are 61 per cent lower than the emissions from fossil fuels.

The United States is the world's biggest bioethanol producer. Bioethanol in the United States is made from corn, which is planted and harvested by machine. Fertilizers are used to improve yields. The farm machinery is powered by fossil fuels, and the process of making fertilizers produces carbon emissions. This means that the overall savings in carbon emissions are much smaller than for Brazilian bioethanol. According to the US Department of Energy, bioethanol made from corn produces carbon emissions that are about 20 per cent lower than the emissions from fossil fuels.

Biofuel problems

Biofuels seem like a perfect replacement for fossil fuels. They absorb carbon dioxide while they are growing, then give it out again when they burn. In theory, they should be carbon neutral.

However, many environmentalists are opposed to replacing fossil fuels with biofuels. This is because in practice, using biofuels is not as straightforward as it seems in theory.

Different in practice

In most cases, growing biofuels produces carbon emissions. Farmers usually use machines to plant the crops and to harvest them. They may also use fertilizer, pesticides, and irrigation (extra watering systems) to get a good crop. All these processes produce carbon emissions.

A second problem is that biofuels are often grown on land that would otherwise be used for food crops. Some biofuel crops, such as corn and sugar cane, are grown as food crops as well as being used for biofuels. This becomes a problem if we want to produce large amounts of biofuels. It will be an even bigger problem as the world population grows, because more people need more food. If we want to grow large amounts of biofuels, there will not be enough fertile land available for growing both food and fuel.

Economic problems

Producing biofuels has had some consequences that perhaps no one expected. Biofuel crops are valuable. They often sell for more money than food crops. Farmers often choose to grow biofuels to make money, not because they are good for the environment. Some farmers have rooted out food crops and planted biofuel crops instead. Others have cleared important habitats such as rainforest and peatlands to grow biofuel crops. In such cases, the benefits of the biofuels are far outweighed by the damage caused to the environment.

> ### Better than diesel
>
> Biodiesel is in many ways a better fuel than diesel oil. It burns more readily than modern diesel fuel, which makes the engine more efficient. It also produces fewer particulates (less soot). Biodiesel is less **corrosive** than normal diesel fuel. This reduces wear and tear on fuel systems.

Second and third generation

Scientists are working on new kinds of biofuel that avoid the problems of the current biofuels. "Second generation" biofuels will be made from crops such as trees and grasses that can grow on land not suitable for growing food. The biofuel will be made from the whole of the plant, not just from starch or plant oils. It is possible to make these kinds of biofuels today, but it is much more expensive than biofuel made from crops such as corn or soybeans.

Biofuels can also be made from microscopic, plant-like **algae**. Some kinds of algae naturally produce oils. If this oil production can be increased enough, they could become a very useful source of biofuels.

Another possibility is to make biofuel from seaweed. Seaweed grows very quickly, and "seaweed farms" would not take up land that could be used to grow food.

An experimental farm in France growing algae in large tanks. The algae contain oils that can be extracted and used as biofuel.

ELECTRICS AND HYBRIDS

Since 1997, many countries have been trying to reduce their carbon emissions to meet their Kyoto Protocol targets. To reduce carbon emissions from transport, governments have tried to make agreements with car manufacturers. In Europe, for example, the European Union asked car manufacturers to reduce vehicle emissions to an average of 120 grams of carbon per kilometre (4 ounces per 1.6 miles).

Some car manufacturers have got close to the emissions targets set for 2012. However, many others have not. Many environmental campaigners think we need new, ambitious targets if we are going to slow down global warming. The group Transport and Environment, for example, suggests we should reduce average car emissions to 80 grams per kilometre (2.8 ounces per mile) by 2020. It will be very difficult to meet these suggested emissions targets with conventional cars. Could electric vehicles be the answer?

How much do they save?

Electric vehicles do not directly produce any carbon emissions. Most electric vehicles may have batteries to provide electric power. These batteries have to be recharged, and this is usually done from the mains. Most of our mains electricity comes from power stations burning fossil fuels. So a large amount of the electricity used to power electric vehicles comes from fossil fuels.

However, a vehicle running on electricity does have some advantages over a vehicle with an internal combustion engine.

- Electric vehicles are quieter than conventional ones.

- Electric vehicles do not need gears.

- Electric motors do not produce emissions directly, so they reduce pollution in busy towns and cities.

- A fossil fuel power station can produce electricity more efficiently than a vehicle engine could use the same fuel. For example, a conventional power station is about 36 to 38 per cent efficient. A combined-cycle power station, which uses gas and steam turbines, can turn 50–60 per cent of its fuel into electricity. An average car engine is only about 20 per cent efficient.

- Not all power stations use fossil fuels. In the United Kingdom, about 30 per cent of electricity is generated from hydroelectricity or other renewable sources.

Shorter range

Perhaps the main disadvantage of battery-powered electric vehicles is that at present they cannot travel as far on a single charge as an engine-powered vehicle can go on a full tank of petrol or diesel. A battery-powered car, for example, has a range of about 160 kilometres (100 miles) on a single charge, while a conventional car might travel 804 kilometres (500 miles) on a full tank.

The battery compartment of a modern electric car. This model is the Peugeot iOn.

Then and Now
Electric vehicles

Electric vehicles are not a new invention. From the 1880s until the early 1900s, electric cars were as popular as those with petrol or diesel engines. They were much quieter and less smelly than early internal combustion cars. From 1898 until 1902, electric cars held the world land speed record. The holder for most of this time was a car called *Le Jamais Contente*, which reached 105.9 kilometres (65.8 miles) per hour. In the early 1900s, petrol became much cheaper and electric cars fell out of fashion. But many trains, and also vehicles such as forklift trucks, are still powered by electricity today.

Slow charging

The big disadvantage of a modern electric vehicle is the time taken to refuel. You can fill up a car fuel tank in a few minutes, but recharging an electric vehicle takes several hours. At present it is also more difficult to recharge an electric vehicle because there are many petrol stations but very few recharging stations.

In recent years, light, powerful batteries have been developed for devices such as laptops and mobile phones. The advances in battery technology have improved batteries for electric cars. But even with these improvements, electric cars are not as cheap and convenient as conventional ones.

Fuel cells and hybrids

Two alternatives to straight battery power are **fuel cells** and **hybrids**. Fuel cells are "batteries" that run on fuel and do not need recharging. A fuel cell can combine hydrogen fuel with oxygen from the air to make electricity. The only waste product from this reaction is water. Cars that run on fuel cells have electric motors, but use fuel like a conventional car. However, at present fuel cells are extremely expensive to make and cannot compete with batteries.

Hybrids are cars powered by a combination of an electric motor and a small IC engine. In most hybrids on the road today, the main power comes from the IC engine. When extra power is needed (for example, when accelerating hard), the electric motor kicks in. The car therefore has the same power as a conventional car with a bigger engine.

Many car manufacturers produce hybrid cars. In general, they have better fuel consumption than similar cars with only IC engines. However, they are more complex mechanically, so they are more expensive to build and to maintain.

Energy from hydrogen?

A fuel cell "burns" hydrogen and oxygen together to produce electricity and water. If the wastewater is collected, it can be converted back to hydrogen and oxygen (this process needs energy). In theory, it would be possible to build a whole energy system on burning hydrogen to get energy and water, then converting the water back to hydrogen fuel. However, there are many problems connected with producing, storing, and using hydrogen.

Efficient batteries

Researchers at the Massachusetts Institute of Technology in the United States may have found an answer to the biggest problem with electric cars – the time they take to charge up. Professor Gerbrand Ceder and student Byoungwoo Kang have discovered that just changing the way of making the material used in the batteries in electric cars can massively reduce charging times. A battery made this way recharges in seconds or minutes, rather than minutes or hours.

This special cutaway engine built for the London Motor Show in 2006 shows the electric motor (right) and petrol engine (left) under the bonnet of a hybrid car.

RETHINKING LIFESTYLES

Designing more efficient engines, using more biofuels, and developing better electric or hybrid vehicles will help to reduce carbon emissions. However, as we have seen, environmentalists have shown that all these technological fixes have problems. They argue that we need to rethink our whole attitude to the way we travel.

Congestion and pollution

The aim of a transport system is to move people and goods from place to place as quickly and easily as possible. In many of the world's biggest cities this just does not happen. There are regular traffic snarl-ups at rush hour, and an accident or other problem can lead to massive hold-ups.

One of the main reasons for this is that shops, offices, and other businesses are concentrated in the centre of cities. Millions of people have to travel into and out of the centre each day to get to work. In many places, people travel to and from the city in their cars because public transport is unreliable or too expensive. Many parents also use cars to take their children to school.

Long-distance travel

Another big use of transport is to move food and other goods around the world. A US study showed that on average, fresh produce such as fruit and vegetables travels almost 1,500 "food miles" (2,400 kilometres) from where it is grown to where it is eventually sold. The transport for these foods uses large amounts of energy and produces tonnes of carbon emissions. Many foods have to be refrigerated in transit in order to stay fresh, and this adds to the energy used during transport.

Environmentalists have led a campaign to persuade people to buy local produce from farm shops and farmers' markets whenever possible. However, it is not always possible to buy some products locally – and in some cases food grown in developing countries, where no machinery or chemicals are used, actually has lower overall carbon emissions than locally grown food.

Crawling cars

The speed limit in many cities is around 40 kilometres (25 miles) per hour. However, congestion in many cities means that cars and other vehicles travel much more slowly than the limit. The slowest city in Europe is London, where the average speed of traffic is just 19 kilometres (12 miles) per hour. The average speed of motor vehicles in Indian cities is about the same. At these speeds, it could actually be quicker to travel by bicycle!

In 1930 (upper photo), the streets of the city of Mumbai, India, were virtually free of traffic. By 2009 (lower photo), traffic levels had increased massively.

Then and Now
India and China

More than one-third of the world's population lives in the Asian countries of India and China. Since 1990, the number of cars in these two countries has skyrocketed. In 2005, India had three times as many cars as in 1990, while in China there were ten times more cars. In many cities, the increase has caused air pollution, traffic congestion, noise, accidents, parking problems, and increased energy use.

Smarter planning

Reorganizing the transport network of a city is a big job. However, some cities have found ways to bring down the amount of travelling people have to do (see the case study on pages 44–47).

One way to bring down the energy costs of transport would be to reduce the distances people travel to work or to school. The best way to do this would be to reorganize our cities. Complete reorganization would be difficult, but it may be possible to use planning laws to ensure a mix of businesses and housing spread across a city, instead of having the businesses concentrated in the centre.

Fewer cars

If vehicles were used more efficiently it would reduce the amount of energy use. For example, there is often only one person travelling in a car – the driver. One way to avoid this is car-pooling, where people who are travelling the same route share a car. Car-pooling is most often used for regular journeys such as school trips or going to and from work. However, it is also possible to use car-pooling for longer trips.

Using more public transport reduces the numbers of private cars on the road and so reduces energy use. Planners in many cities have tried many ways to do this. One of the simplest is to make sure that bus, tram, and train services are regular, cheap, and do not get held up in traffic. Special bus or tram lanes are often created. Many cities have park-and-ride schemes, where drivers leave their cars in car parks on the edge of a city, then travel into town on public transport.

One scheme for reducing the traffic in a city centre is "congestion charging". Private vehicles have to pay to drive in the most congested parts of a city. Congestion charging has been introduced in cities such as London, where many people have switched to public transport in order to avoid paying the fee.

Perhaps one of the best ways to reduce the energy costs of transport is not to use motor vehicles at all. Over half of all car journeys are less than five miles. Trips of this length could be done on a bicycle.

Personal rapid transit

Personal rapid transit (PRT) is an experimental kind of transport with many of the advantages of a car but the energy savings of public transport. A PRT system has small, lightweight vehicles controlled by computer that run on fixed tracks. Passengers board at set stations, but generally they will not have to wait; the car will already be waiting. Unlike a bus, it can go directly to the passenger's destination without stopping on the way. A few small PRT systems have already been built – for example, the ULTra PRT at Heathrow Airport. However, more work needs to be done before a large PRT network can be created.

Cellular city design

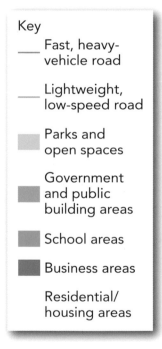

Key

___ Fast, heavy-vehicle road

___ Lightweight, low-speed road

Parks and open spaces

Government and public building areas

School areas

Business areas

Residential/housing areas

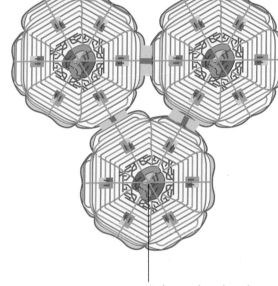

Hub, with schools, businesses, and government buildings

A plan showing how towns and cities could be reorganized to cut transport costs. It consists of a series of "cells", each with a central business and government centre. Fast roads carrying heavy traffic radiate out from the centre, with slower, lighter traffic on roads connecting these radiating roads.

ENVIRONMENTALISM IN ACTION

Two traffic solutions

Two cities, one in Brazil in South America and one in the United States, have designed very different solutions to their transport problems.

Curitiba, Brazil

In the 1960s, the city of Curitiba was growing fast, causing many problems. There was traffic chaos and pollution. Many poor people lived in slums where there was no water, electricity, or drains. The city needed a plan for improvement. The council decided to hold a competition to find ways to solve the city's problems. A group of architects was given the job of turning the best ideas from the competition into concrete plans.

At the heart of the improvement plan was a new transport network. Five major roads were built radiating out from the city centre like the spokes of a wheel. Each road has three parts. On one side, the traffic moves towards town; on the other side, it moves outwards. Between the two is a two-way road that can be used only by the city's rapid transit system. This is a fleet of buses that can each carry 270 people.

A rapid bus stops at a station of the Bus Rapid Transit (BRT) system in Curitiba, Brazil.

The buses run every few minutes. The bus stops are long, tubular shelters where people can board very quickly. The fare is the same from any part of the city. The rapid transit buses stop on the edge of the city centre, because only pedestrians are allowed in the centre itself. In addition to the rapid transit buses, there are local buses that operate in the areas between the radiating "spokes".

Because the bus services in the city are so good, 85 per cent of people use public transport to travel around the city. This means that other traffic on the roads is much lighter than in other cities. The large rapid transit buses use far less fuel per passenger than private cars, so the transport system produces fewer carbon emissions. Fuel use is 30 per cent less than in other, similar Brazilian cities.

A green success

Curitiba is a great example of how planning can benefit everyone. It has a superb transport system, but some areas in the centre are closed to traffic, to make pleasant pedestrian areas. There are many parks and other green spaces, and an excellent waste recycling system. In 2007, Curitiba was voted one of the greenest cities in the world.

The Curitiba city plan was a "big idea" for change that really worked. But big ideas do not always turn out so well...

Other environmental initiatives

The transport system is not the only way in which planning in Curitiba is environmentally friendly. Some areas in the city have been protected from future development and have been turned into parks. Curitiba also set up a major recycling system well before it was used in other cities – recycling organic waste, plastic, glass, and metal.

Boston, USA

In the early 1970s the city of Boston in the United States had big traffic problems. The centre of the city was split in two by a six-lane raised expressway. The road was old and needed replacing. It was always congested because traffic going from north to south and from east to west had to use the same stretch of road. The constant traffic produced large amounts of noise and air pollution in the city centre.

Boston's governor and head of transport together came up with a plan to replace the expressway with a tunnel 3.5 miles (5.6 kilometres) long right under the city centre. The tunnel was just one part of "The Big Dig" – a huge engineering project that also involved building a new bridge and two underwater tunnels.

The Big Dig

The Big Dig was a very expensive project and was plagued with problems. There were leaks in the underwater tunnels and problems with the concrete being used. Four workers were killed in construction accidents. The project took over 20 years to complete and cost at least £9 billion. It will take the city until at least 2038 to pay off these costs.

When the Big Dig was completed in 2006, traffic flowed much more freely through the city. The central tunnel greatly reduced above-ground traffic in the city centre and the area where the expressway had been became parkland. As a result, the centre of Boston became a more pleasant place.

A tale of two cities

Although it has reduced traffic congestion, the Big Dig has not reduced the overall amount of traffic through the city – and it has not cut down on carbon emissions or fossil fuel use. By contrast, the transport system in Curitiba has produced real reductions in carbon emissions.

Environmental campaigners see the Big Dig as a planning failure. The scheme cost much more than was originally planned. This is mainly because it was a huge, complicated project that led to many mistakes and accidents. The transport system built in Curitiba was much more straightforward, so it cost far less.

Most of the environmentally friendly parts of the original Big Dig plan were dropped. A rail link between the north and south of the city, which would have greatly reduced car use, was not built. Many parks, footpaths, cycle tracks, and pedestrian bridges were not completed. In Curitiba, "green" ideas were at the centre of the plans for the city.

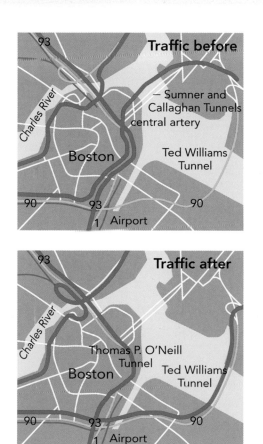

These maps show how the Big Dig changed roads in central Boston. Traffic travelling from east to west has been diverted out of the city centre on Route 90, while north-to-south traffic on Route 93 now travels under the city centre in the Thomas P. O'Neill Tunnel.

Signposts for the future

Since the 1970s, environmentalists, governments, and businesses across the world have tried to reduce carbon emissions and find alternatives to fossil fuels. But progress has been slow. For example, the first experiments with electric cars happened in the 19th century, but electric cars are still a tiny minority of overall car sales. So what will happen in the future?

Do we need cars?

Some environmentalists think that the only way we will solve our transport problems is to give up cars altogether. This seems unlikely to happen in the near future. People can do things in cars that would be much more difficult using other forms of transport. They can go on a trip when they like, take far more luggage than they could carry on public transport, and drive directly to their destination without having to stop at other places on the way. However, we have seen that with careful planning, it is possible to create cities where people do not have to travel far to get to work or to do their shopping. Good public transport, pleasant footpaths, and safe cycle routes can also help to reduce the need for cars.

Future power

Cars are unlikely to disappear in the near future. However, the way they are powered may change. They may use third-generation biofuels made from algae or seaweed, or they might run on batteries. Eventually, cars could be part of an economy in which hydrogen-powered fuel cells produce water as waste that is then turned back into hydrogen using solar power. We will need to consider all these new kinds of power (and other new ones) to replace fossil fuels.

Saving energy

Cars are very heavy compared to the people they carry. The average US car weighs about 2,000 kilograms (4,400 pounds). Even with four people on board, 86 per cent of the car's fuel is used to move the car itself. If we made cars smaller and lighter, this would produce big energy savings. Until recently, studies suggested that smaller, lighter cars were not as safe as large, heavy cars. However, more recent studies have shown that they are just as safe. So cars in the future are likely to be lighter.

Cars, trains, and other vehicles are expensive to manufacture in terms of price, but also in terms of energy. One way to retrieve some of this energy is to recycle the vehicle parts. The interiors of these railway cars are made from 97 per cent recyclable materials.

Lighter, greener cars

Lighter cars with low emissions look set to become a reality within a few years. The German manufacturer Audi are building an affordable, compact car with an aluminium body that keeps the weight down. Another German manufacturer, BMW, is developing a range of electric and hybrid cars with carbon-fibre bodies. In the United States, engineers at the Massachusetts Institute of Technology have designed a small, two-seater city car that weighs less than 1,000 kilograms (2,200 pounds) and can "fold up" to fit into a space of only 1.5 metres (5 feet) in length.

Powering ships and boats

Many of the advances in technology that have been developed for cars could also work for ships and boats. Boat engines could, for example, use biofuels in the same way that car engines can.

One development that is promising for powering ships is pod propulsion. Instead of being connected to the ship's engines by long shafts, the propellers are in "pods" slung below the hull. Pod systems can be built so that the whole unit can turn to point the propeller in a different direction. This means that the ship can steer using the pod units, and does not need a rudder.

Propellers on pods below the hull give better streamlining, which saves energy. Having no rudder also reduces **drag** and saves more energy.

Using less energy on water

Land vehicles only have to move through air, which offers a lot less resistance than water. Future boats may use ideas currently being researched that aim to cut the drag of a boat hull by pumping air underneath it. Air cavity system (ACS) boats have a wedge-shaped cavity in the boat hull that is designed to trap air pumped into it. The air acts as a lubricating layer between the boat and the water. In experimental boats, ACS has cut drag by between 15 and 40 per cent. ACS could allow future boats to travel at speeds of up to 50 knots (93 kilometres per hour) without huge rises in fuel consumption.

In some pod systems, the propellers are driven by an electric motor in the pod. Engines on board ship generate the electricity. This system is more efficient than driving the propellers directly by using engines.

Future air transport

Until recently, the main improvement in aircraft carbon emissions came from improvements in engine design (see page 27). However, the first airliners to use biofuel flew in 2011 (see page 31), and many future aircraft will probably run at least partly on biofuel.

There are many ideas for powering aircraft further into the future. There are several kinds of hybrid aircraft being developed. Some, like road hybrids, are conventional aircraft that have both an internal combustion engine and an electric motor. But the Lockheed-Martin P-791 is another kind of hybrid – a hybrid airship. It is heavier than air, so it does not actually float, but takes off and lands like an aircraft. However, the aircraft includes three giant cells filled with the very light gas helium, like an airship. This makes the aircraft very buoyant and means it needs far less fuel to fly. Hybrids like this could stay airborne for many weeks and carry large loads.

> ### Wind power
>
> Future ships may use wind power to reduce fuel use. In 2008, the cargo ship MS *Beluga* made a two-week trip from Germany to Venezuela using a giant kite to help it along. The kite is similar to the parafoils used by kite surfers, but much bigger – about the area of a football pitch. On days when the wind is strong enough, the kite can reduce a ship's fuel consumption by an average of 10–15 per cent.

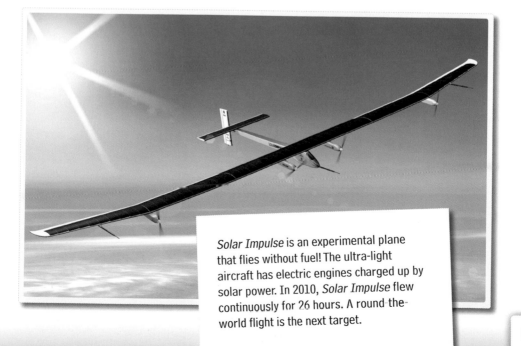

Solar Impulse is an experimental plane that flies without fuel! The ultra-light aircraft has electric engines charged up by solar power. In 2010, *Solar Impulse* flew continuously for 26 hours. A round-the-world flight is the next target.

ENVIRONMENTALISM IN ACTION

A city for tomorrow?

Masdar is a new city being built in the desert, close to the city of Abu Dhabi. The whole city is an experiment in green planning and technology. The aim of the project is to use 50 per cent less energy than in a conventional city of a similar size. When completed in 2025, Masdar will be home to about 50,000 people.

The layout and design of Masdar aims to make it comfortable to live in the buildings and walk the streets even when the sun is burning down on the desert. The buildings are close together and the streets are narrow, with overhanging roofs to provide shade. The whole city is walled, which provides more protection from the desert heat. The design is good for walking, but perhaps not so good for other kinds of transport.

No internal combustion cars will be allowed in Masdar. All vehicles within the city will be electric. The electricity will come mainly from solar power stations in the desert close to the city, so the carbon emissions due to transport will be very low.

An artist's impression of how Masdar will look from the air once it is finished.

In the original plan for Masdar, the city's transport network was going to be below ground. A PRT system using 3,000 driverless cars was designed to be a kind of green taxi service that would deliver the customer directly to their destination 24 hours per day. A pilot project using 16 cars worked well and is still operating. However, the cost of the complete system was too high, so the idea has been dropped. Instead, transport will consist of electric buses and cars, plus two railway networks running from Abu Dhabi to the centre of Masdar.

Although Masdar's transport system will not be as futuristic as originally planned, the design of the city still points to the future. People visiting Masdar will arrive in high-speed transport (such as trains) or conventional cars. In the city itself, there will be a different transport system that produces no pollution and little noise. This will greatly reduce carbon emissions and keep the air in Masdar fresh.

Masdar facts

Where: Abu Dhabi, United Arab Emirates

Area: 6 square kilometres (2.3 square miles)

Population (expected): 45,000–50,000

Aim: To build a sustainable city relying entirely on renewable energy that uses only half the energy of a normal city of similar size.

Project begun: 2006

Completion (expected): 2025

Cost (estimated): £11.6 billion ($19 billion)

Designers: Norman Foster & Partners

Owners: Abu Dhabi Future Energy Company

"Only use energy when you have exhausted design."

Motto of architects from Norman Foster & Partners

ENVIRONMENTALISM IN ACTION

Testing new ideas

When scientists and engineers come up with new ideas, they have to find ways to test them in the real world. One way of doing this is through challenge events.

World Solar Challenge

The World Solar Challenge is a test of speed and endurance for cars powered entirely by the Sun. The Challenge is a race across the centre of Australia, from Darwin in the north to Adelaide in the south. The total distance is 3,000 kilometres (about 1,860 miles). Most entries are cars built at universities and colleges. The cars are driven by electric motors, and the upper surface is covered with solar cells to provide the electricity. The cells are also used to charge the car's batteries.

In 2005, the winning car, *Nuna 3*, averaged a scorching 103 kilometres (64 miles) per hour. This was the fastest Solar Challenge car to date.

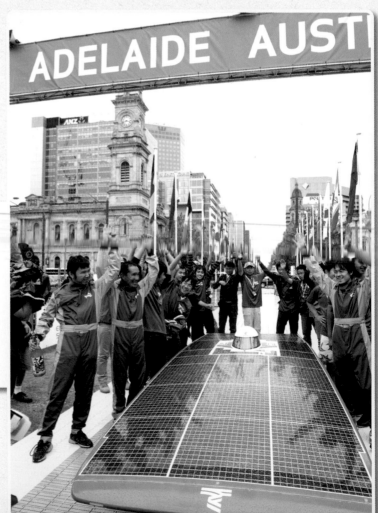

There are the Japanese winners celebrating victory at the finishing line of the 2010 World Solar Challenge with their solar car, Tokai Challenge.

Shell Eco-Marathon

Three Shell Eco-Marathons are held each year in Europe, the United States, and Asia. The idea is not to see who can go fastest, but who can go furthest on a litre of fuel (or on 1 kilowatt-hour of electricity).

The record for the most fuel-efficient car of all was set in 2005 by *PAC-Car II*, designed and built by Team ETH from Switzerland. *PAC-Car II* weighed only 29 kilograms (64 pounds). It was powered by a fuel cell that ran on hydrogen. In the 2005 race, it clocked a fuel consumption of 5,385 kilometres (3,346 miles) per litre of fuel. The car could drive from London to Moscow in Russia and back and still have fuel in the tank!

Car design

The cars taking part in the World Solar Challenge and the Shell Eco-Marathon are not practical. In most, there is only room for the driver, who has to lie almost flat and has a very limited view. But to win the challenges, design teams push the cars and materials to the limits.

Solar speed

The very first World Solar Challenge race in 1987 was won by a solar-powered car called *Sunraycer*, entered by a team from the US car maker General Motors. *Sunraycer* was much faster than the other cars in the race. It arrived in Adelaide a whole two days before the second-place car! It also set a speed record of 121.145 kilometres (75.276 miles) per hour for a car powered only by the Sun (without batteries).

Sunraycer's speed record stood for 23 years. It was broken in 2011 by a car called *Sunswift IV*, or "*IVy*" for short. *IVy* was built by a team of students and staff from the University of New South Wales in Sydney, Australia. In January 2011, *IVy* reached a new world record speed of 142.5 kilometres (88.5 miles) per hour. This was over 21 kilometres (13 miles) per hour faster than *Sunraycer*.

WHAT HAVE WE LEARNED?

Since the 1960s, environmentalism has grown into a worldwide movement. By the 1990s, the impact of environmentalism led to the setting up of the United Nations Earth Summits and targets for reducing carbon emissions. However, the impact of environmentalism on our transport systems has been limited.

In most countries, the main focus of effort is on trying to make cars more environment-friendly. This makes some sense, because cars produce more emissions than any other form of transport. However, environmentalists believe that this will not produce large reductions in carbon emissions. Even if we do improve the carbon emissions of cars, they will still use more energy than public transport, bicycles, or walking. In this area, the environmental point of view has not had a strong impact.

Sustainable transport

For truly sustainable transport systems, environmentalists argue, we need to change our whole attitude to travel and transport. We need to reorganize our lifestyles so that we live nearer to where we work and do our shopping. We need to improve our public transport systems so that we use private vehicles far less. Future PRT electric-vehicle networks could provide a public transport system with many of the advantages of private cars.

Keeping things moving

The arguments of environmentalists have had less impact on transport than they have had in other areas, such as energy production. However, environmental arguments do have important effects. Changes to our transport systems involve difficult decisions that are often unpopular. For that reason, politicians and governments often avoid or put off making these kinds of difficult decisions. However, as was found with congestion charging in the city of London (see page 42), these kinds of decisions can produce real benefits in the longer term. Environmentalists can help to keep the focus on why such changes are important.

The need to change our attitudes to transport has become urgent. In 1990, the total world carbon emissions were 21,563 tonnes. If we carry on as we are, then by 2025 emissions will have reached 37,124 tonnes. Yet scientists believe that we need to reduce emissions well below 1990 levels by 2050 to prevent serious global environmental damage. We do not have much time.

The best sustainable transport of all is a bike! These bicycle taxis operating in Sydney, Australia, also have a small electric motor to help get them up hills.

Discussion panel: will it happen?

The basic problem is simple: we need to change our transport systems, to use fossil fuels less, and to reduce carbon emissions. We have known about the problem for around 40 years. We know of many ways to reduce energy use, and we now have the technology that could partly replace fossil fuels, and yet we have made very little progress towards developing sustainable transport. Environmentalists have done an excellent job of alerting the world to the dangers of pollution and global warming, but the decisions that will really change things for the better have to be made by politicians from different countries working together. Will governments manage to do this before it is too late? The answer is in the balance.

TIMELINE

1820 World population reaches 1 billion.

1839 First crude fuel cell is developed by Welsh scientist William Grove.

1864 George Perkins Marsh publishes his book *Man and Nature*.

1885 John Stanley begins selling the Rover safety bicycle – the first modern bicycle.

1890 Work of John Muir helps to establish the Yosemite and Sequoia national parks in California.

1899 Belgian Camille Jenatzy's electric car, *La Jamais Contente*, becomes the fastest car in the world. It travels at nearly 106 kilometres (66 miles) per hour.

1900 At the World's Fair, Rudolf Diesel runs his engine on pure peanut oil.
Belgian car manufacturer Pieper introduces a car powered by a combination of a small petrol engine and an electric motor. This is one of the first ever hybrid car designs.

1921 Thomas Midgley, Jr discovers that a chemical containing lead works well to stop "knocking" (mistimed explosions) in petrol engines. His invention is very successful, but causes lead pollution in the atmosphere for 50 years or more.

1930 World population reaches 2 billion.

1930s 1960s UK inventor Francis Thomas Bacon develops first practical fuel cell.

1939 The Shell Eco-Marathon starts out as a bet between scientists as to who can get the most miles per gallon from a car.

1952 The Great London Smog alerts British people to the dangers of air pollution.

1956 The Clean Air Act is introduced in the United Kingdom to reduce pollution from fires and smoke.

1958 Mauna Loa Observatory in Hawaii begins monitoring the levels of carbon dioxide in the atmosphere. Over time, the data shows a clear rise in carbon dioxide levels.

1962 Rachel Carson's book *Silent Spring* is published.

1963 First of a series of Clean Air Acts in the United States that are designed to reduce pollution from cars as well as fires.

1968 Curitiba begins its Master Plan to reorganize the transport system.

1969 The Cuyahoga River in Ohio, USA catches fire because there is so much pollution in the water.

1970 First Earth Day events are held across the United States.

1973 Brazil begins making bioethanol from sugar cane. Mass production of biofuel cars begins in 1979.
First oil crisis occurs as oil prices rise steeply.

1974 World population reaches 4 billion.

1987 World Solar Challenge race across Australia is run for the first time. It offers a showcase for solar-powered cars.
The Brundtland Report, *Our Common Future*, talks about sustainable development.

1991 The Boston Big Dig begins.

1992 UN Earth Summit held in Rio de Janeiro, Brazil, from 3 to 14 June.

1999 World population reaches 6 billion.

2003 London introduces congestion charging.

2006 First airline flight that is fuelled by biofuel.

2008 Pratt & Whitney produce the Pratt & Whitney PurePower® engine, their first geared turbofan engine.

2010 The solar-powered aircraft *Solar Impulse* flies for over 26 hours powered only by sunlight.

2011 World population reaches 7 billion.

GLOSSARY

abattoir place where animals are killed for eating

acid rain rain caused by air pollution that damages forests and harms wildlife in rivers and lakes

algae plant-like living things found in all kinds of water. Algae range in size from microscopic organisms to huge seaweeds.

biodegradable can be broken down in the environment into very simple chemicals

biofuel fuel made either from plant materials or animal waste

biomaterial plastic or other synthetic material made from plants

climate change shift in weather patterns, frequency of extreme weather events, and average temperatures caused by global warming

congestion road blockage caused by too much traffic

corrosive causing damage by a chemical process when in contact with other materials

drag resistance to the movement of something

ecology study of the interactions between living things and their environment

efficient produces an amount of work that is close to the amount of energy put into it. Most engines can turn only about 25 per cent of the energy in the fuel into useful work.

emissions production and releasing of gas

fermenting turning a liquid into alcohol

fossil fuel naturally occurring fuel, usually found below ground or under the seabed, that takes millions of years to form. Coal, crude oil, and natural gas are the three major fossil fuels.

fuel cell device that uses hydrogen or a similar fuel, plus oxygen from the air, to produce electricity directly

global warming gradual rise in Earth's average temperature caused by increase in greenhouse gases in the atmosphere

goods things that people manufacture (make) and sell

greenhouse gas gas that stores heat in the atmosphere. Carbon dioxide and methane are examples of greenhouse gases.

habitat place where particular living things normally live

hybrid car powered by a combination of an electric motor and a small internal combustion engine

hydrocarbon chemical compound containing only carbon and hydrogen

incandescent light bulb bulb with a brightly glowing filament. It was the main kind of bulb used in homes for over 100 years, but it is now being replaced by low-energy bulbs.

internal combustion (IC) engine engine in which combustion (burning) is produced by causing an explosion of a mixture of fuel and air inside a small chamber called a cylinder

kinetic energy movement energy

oxide chemical compound produced when oxygen reacts with an element or other chemical

pesticide chemical sprayed on farm crops to kill insects or other pests that eat the crop

renewable can be replaced. Wood is a renewable fuel because new trees can be grown to replace those used as fuel.

smog choking mix of smoke and fog only usually found in cities

starch a type of carbohydrate used by most plants as a food store

sustainable does not use up too many natural resources or pollute the environment

turbojet jet engine in which the jet gases also operate a turbine-driven compressor

FIND OUT MORE

Books

Cities (Sustaining our Environment), Jill Laidlaw (Franklin Watts, 2009)

Designing Greener Vehicles and Buildings (Why Science Matters), Andrew Solway (Heinemann Library, 2008)

Sustainable Transportation (How Can We Save Our World?), Cath Senker (Arcturus Publishing, 2009)

Transport (Maps of the Environmental World), Meg and Jack Gillett (Wayland, 2011)

Transport (Sustainable World), Rob Bowden (Wayland, 2007)

Websites

Earth Day: the History of a Movement:
www.earthday.org/earth-day-history-movement
Information on the history of Earth Days and a video of the first Earth Day event.

Earth Summit 2012: **www.uncsd2012.org/rio20**
The website for the latest meeting of the United Nations Conference on Sustainable Development.

Shell Eco-Marathon: **www.shell.com/home/content/ecomarathon**
Events held around the world each year to find the most fuel-efficient vehicle in the world.

What Car: Green Cars: **www.whatcar.com/green-cars**
A guide to the most fuel-efficient modern cars.

World Solar Challenge: **www.worldsolarchallenge.org**
The website of the annual solar-powered car race across Australia.

The World's Worst Traffic Jams:
www.time.com/time/world/article/0,8599,1733872,00.html
An article in *Time* magazine about traffic congestion around the world.

DVDs

Earth Days (PBS, 2009). A documentary made by the US Public Broadcasting Service about the first Earth Day and the start of the environmental movement in the United States.

Organizations

Sustrans
2 Cathedral Square
College Green
Bristol BS1 5DD
www.sustrans.org.uk
Sustrans is short for "sustainable transport". The organization sets up
cycle routes and does other work to encourage more walking and cycling.

Earth Day Network
1616 P St. NW
Suite 340
Washington, DC 20036
USA
www.earthday.org
Earth Day Network works with many partners to mobilize the
environmental movement. More than 1 billion people now participate
in Earth Day activities each year.

Friends of the Earth
26–28 Underwood Street
London N1 7JQ
www.foe.co.uk
One of the first environmental organizations to campaign for reduction
of carbon emissions and prevention of climate change.

United Nations Environment Programme
www.unep.org
The UN organization concerned with reducing carbon emissions and
protecting the environment.

Other topics to research

Look at the information on the food in your house. How far has the food
travelled? Research how you could reduce food miles. Are there local
farmers' markets in your area? What foods are grown or made locally?

Write a transport diary. How many trips do you do by car each week?
Do some research to find out how much carbon your trips emit. Are
there ways in which you could reduce these emissions?

INDEX